DISCARDED

☆

**OUT OF THIS NETTLE,
DANGER . . .**

Essays for the Post-War Era

☆

Out of this nettle, danger, we pluck this flower, safety.—HENRY IV, PART 1

OUT OF THIS NETTLE, DANGER...

BY HAROLD W. DODDS

Essay Index Reprint Series

BOOKS FOR LIBRARIES PRESS
FREEPORT, NEW YORK

Copyright 1943 by Princeton University Press

Reprinted 1969 by arrangement

STANDARD BOOK NUMBER:
8369-1406-6

LIBRARY OF CONGRESS CATALOG CARD NUMBER:
78-99631

PRINTED IN THE UNITED STATES OF AMERICA

CONTENTS

I.	TRUSTEES OF THE AMERICAN DREAM	1
II.	COMING: AN AGE OF FRESH OPPORTUNITY	4
III.	TOWARD A DURABLE PEACE	9
IV.	THE ANATOMY OF COURAGE	15
V.	FREEDOM AND RESPONSIBILITY	19
VI.	THE CASE FOR LIBERALISM	25
VII.	"HE THAT'S SECURE IS NOT SAFE"	31
VIII.	DEMOCRACY'S CHALLENGE TO PRIVATE AND COMMUNITY ENTERPRISE	36
IX.	EDUCATION FOR USE	46

I. TRUSTEES OF THE AMERICAN DREAM

THROUGHOUT the fabric of our national life has run the golden thread of a radiant dream of what America might become. We today, familiar with the conventional language in which it is expressed, can scarcely realize its revolutionary significance to those early settlers on our shores who came in search of liberty and opportunity in a free land. Because it is most readily expressed in economic terms its deeper meaning in terms of personality and spirit is too often obscured. This dream has never been realized; sometimes it has been perverted, but it has never been discredited or abandoned. In these days we must recapture all its strength and inspiration. The nation must rely upon its young people to keep faith with this dream by work and vision which alone will bring it to pass. On their shoulders rests the trusteeship for its fulfillment.

Having offered the heavy sacrifices which are being asked of them today, the younger generation will return to the ways of peace with authority to make our country what they wish it to be. They will have the votes to make their will prevail. Especially will our college graduates be able to exert an influence out of all proportion to their numbers if they accept the labor and responsibility of leadership.

It is therefore important that college men, especially, understand the nature of that leadership to which they will be called. It is an old saying that intelligent and courageous leadership is more necessary under democracy than under any other form of government. Yet, except in times of great national emergency, popular American views of democracy have leaned to the notion that "we the people" have no need of leaders. We tend to forget that the key to democracy is not to be found in the capacity of the voters to govern themselves without leaders, but in the opportunity to utilize leadership wherever it shows itself in every element of society. In contrast to other systems of government, leaders in a democracy have to gain leadership in their own right, and this is as it should be. Democracy will survive only in proportion to the wisdom with which it selects and follows its leaders, and discards them when they cease to embody the popular will. Democracy's first duty, therefore, is to preserve a social mobility by which the channels of supply of new leaders will always be open, while requiring that the leaders prove themselves continuously on a strictly democratic basis. We must never think of a leader as other than one of ourselves; we must never fail to remember that he is a leader solely by our appointment.

When the evil thing we are now fighting has been destroyed, may our young college men come back, resolved to continue to give themselves to the service of the state. Some—a larger number, I hope, than in the past—will enter public life as administrators or politicians. (No one need be afraid of the name "politician." They may call him a statesman after he is dead.) All of them will have opportunities for service in civic and non-governmental capacities. Every business and profession can be made a channel of service to the nation. Indeed, business will require statesmanship of a high order.

Because of the special privileges college men have enjoyed, democracy has a right to expect that they will return to her payments in public service beyond what the tax collector can exact. Because they have been beneficiaries of special privileges they will not be completely happy unless they do so. Truly satisfying success will come in the post-war period only to him who accepts continuing social responsibilities, rejecting the egocentric view and finding tasks in life which express moral aims higher than his own personal comfort or individual welfare. Only by so doing can he be certain of avoiding the blight of frustration, the sense of emptiness and failure—the feeling of being stuck, which before the war had become so common as to be described as the general neurosis of the day.

The college man will find that his education will be valid in the post-war era because it rests on timeless values. No political system so well expresses man's acceptance of those values as that under which we live. We are not fighting for a new order. We are fighting for a world in which America can chart her future progress as a projection of the curve which her history has already plotted. Mr. John G. Winant has expressed this truth in eloquent phrases: "We must be great of purpose or we cannot survive. We are fighting to win a second chance to make the greatest of traditions come true. Do not let us ever talk as if we were fighting to substitute something else for that tradition; because there is nothing to substitute. Either we go ahead, perfecting the political and moral system we have inherited, or we let the system perish and the world revert to barbarism."

Here in a few words is presented the ideal of the past and the tested basis for the future of America. Our fighting men will be at home when they return to her to resume the occupations of peace, for she will be at bottom the same America to which we have owned allegiance all along. With their help she will go ahead, perfecting the tradition we have inherited.

☆ ☆

II. COMING: AN AGE OF FRESH OPPORTUNITY

Pessimism is frequently a rationalization of one's own weaknesses. When young men think about the future, they will do well to turn a deaf ear to defeatists whose gloom usually reflects their own inability to keep pace with life or to visualize the possibilities inherent in changing conditions. The youth of America face heavy and grim responsibilities in this war. Let them never succumb to prophets of despair; let them never doubt that when these responsibilities have finally been discharged they will find an unparalleled chance to build a more harmonious and fruitful America on a basis more sound and permanent than we have yet known. Remember that dynamic moments of history open up new frontiers of opportunity. Despite the fact that the outlook at the moment may seem forbidding, today's disorder will usher in an age of fresh opportunity for young people, if they will it hard enough.

In counselling against pessimism I am not promising ease and material comfort. We know now that the shallow optimism of the past, which erroneously assured such a rosy future through the evolution of man's natural instincts for goodness without struggle on his part, prepared us poorly for the realities of life. Let us be prepared for a realistic world, but let us not surrender to the conviction that we cannot, if we will, reconstruct an America of opportunity.

There is historical evidence that disturbed epochs of the past have been creative epochs as well. I realize that we are apt to read into the record of past events the meanings which we wish them to have; but I believe nevertheless that the general proposition just recited is sound.

For example, historians tell us that the end of the Middle Ages was characterized by disorder, deep dejection and universal pessimism. Yet we know now that the Renaissance was just around the corner, preparing to throw off the ecclesiastical and feudal despotism of centuries.

The English Revolution of the seventeenth century coincided with an era of disintegration of accepted customs in politics, economics and religion. Many men of the time who saw their familiar and prosperous world crumbling about them must have viewed the event with grave misgivings and fears. Yet a great yeast was at work, says John Buchan, which, surviving the disorder of revolution, worked for human betterment and freedom, and America at once became a direct beneficiary of it.

The French Revolution gave birth to terror, disorder and world wars. Supported by a victory-intoxicated nation, Napoleon was able to disturb the peace of the world for years and to threaten the liberties of all Europe. For two years England lived in almost daily expectation of invasion by a militarist whose reputation for success had become legendary. There were ample grounds for dark pessimism in those days when Napoleon's yoke threatened. Yet the idealism of the Revolution, embodied in the slogan of liberty, equality and fraternity, survived the evils of hate and fear; and the period that followed was marked by the expansion of democracy and opportunity throughout the civilized world.

These historical examples are not offered as exact parallels to the present era. Two of them involved costly armed revolutions, repetitions of which are unnecessary for politically mature peoples. America, once it has succeeded, in collaboration with its allies, in resisting the change through violence proposed by the Axis, will be able to proceed with its plans to perfect the civilization it has inherited by the peaceful changes of seasoned democratic processes. The historical examples I have cited serve merely to demonstrate the general proposition that periods of disturbance may be transformed into epochs distinguished for human advancement.

If we in America are passing through a moment of more rapid evolution than usual, in which our democratic institutions are serving as the instruments of change, the final course of that evolution will be guided by young people who are now fighting the Axis aggressors. If we are at the end of a phase, then by the same token we are at the beginning of another; and the future is theirs. There is no reason, therefore, for youth to be dejected about the future.

This present hour of trial by battle, in which we must first prevail, can serve as a preparation for a fresh start. At this moment our nation may be clearing the stage for a new drama of American life that will portray the American dream more accurately than any in our history. It will be an exciting and satisfying time to be alive. But first there will be some accumulated rubbish to sweep away.

For example, one serious error that has injured the tone of the past generation, a peculiarly all-embracing materialism, must be corrected. This error has taken various forms, some of them highly philosophical and abstract. It has not been confined to raw preoccupation with worldly goods. Money grubbers and profiteers have not been the only guilty ones. Belief in the primacy of material goods has infected wide areas of thought in recent years. It led some sincere humanitarians to accept a lopsided economic interpretation of history. The doctrine that human values are but reflections of economic forces has distorted our attitudes more than we are generally aware. Some even have exhorted us to believe that economic betterment and wider distribution of wealth is about all that there is to religion.

I do not mean to say that economic welfare will not always be important. Certainly I am not arguing against reforms which spell higher standards of living for the less privileged or wider distribution of cultural opportunities and advantages. What I do assert is that any philosophy of life is evil that does not recognize the inescapable opposition between the material and the spiritual that runs through all human experience. Such a philosophy is evil because it is untrue.

Another variant of the general materialism that afflicted the United States was the comfortable doctrine that spirituality and business success were but two sides of the same shield. Be good and you will prosper can easily be made to mean that whatever prospers is good. It was pleasant to know that religion was good business; that if you were right with God your affairs were bound to flourish.

These various manifestations of materialism, whether issuing from the pulpit or from the chamber of commerce, were rooted in a single comprehensive fallacy that was draining America of its faith in ideals and its will to sacrifice. Belief that human perfection can be attained through economics was thinning our blood.

"Shall we be a prosperous nation after the war?" The question is natural but is it really of first importance? The stern historical truth seems to be that prosperity does not develop strength of character; nor have prosperous eras been characterized by the dominance of the highest human qualities and aspirations. Circumstances of ease and safety are far more dangerous than we think. If the war purges our souls through suffering and work for a common cause, success in the years of peaceful reconstruction to follow will come to those who worry less about prosperity for themselves and more about the satisfactions of self-expression not for oneself but for others.

Our deficiencies have not been in the region of knowledge or science. Our failures have been due to lack of sufficient wisdom and will power to trust our highest aspirations and to link them to our knowledge and science. Even in respect to economics and politics we have been unwilling to utilize what we know, fragmentary and piecemeal though it be, because to do so would have involved what appeared to be a sacrifice of our short-term interests or a risk to our vested security. Our outlook was narrow and self-defeating because we had forgotten to pay sufficient consideration to those higher faculties of man that mark him off from the animal. We assimilated goodness to our own shortsighted preference for material welfare and we elected to enjoy freedom without discipline. To paraphrase Emerson, things were in the saddle and were riding mankind.

We are beginning to learn anew in this country that the quality of our civilization is not determined so much by things as by beliefs, by what the people believe to be true and what they believe to be false. Belief in truth is a matter of faith as well as knowledge. Although many moralists and scholars have tried to divorce truth from religious ideas and affiliations, it remains rooted in religion. The fact is that the values which democracy embodies, which America at her best accepts as her own, were first expressed through religion. We shall go astray to our own hurt if we forget that the basis of judgment between true and false originated in religion and will continue to be religious.

In conclusion, one important qualification must be made to the basic optimism which this chapter expresses. If we cannot organize the nations for peace; if after this war we must continue on a war basis, economically and psychologically, as we undoubtedly shall unless we can establish a durable peace, the future of the American dream is dark. The next chapter presents the case for organized international collaboration, which alone can supply an atmosphere favorable to it.

☆ ☆ ☆

III. TOWARD A DURABLE PEACE

IF WE are not to be frustrated once again, the desire for a durable peace which stirs the hearts of most men and women throughout the civilized world must this time be implemented by some institutional arrangement for international collaboration that will conform to men's emotional loyalties as well as appeal to their intellects. The fact that our behavior stems so largely from our emotions must enter into all plans for peace. An international order adequate to the situation will therefore be difficult to achieve but it is possible of attainment if we will it hard enough. War is irrational and illogical. International order based on the moral idea of reign of law is rational and logical, but its fulfillment calls for a supreme act of will and the submergence of some narrow aims and ideals in a larger concept of America's future welfare. One encouraging fact is that the war has brought clarification and a renewed respect for those moral values which alone can form the basis of a just and durable peace.

Ten years ago my generation was wont to deplore the cynicism which seemed to be sapping the strength of youth. Heaven knows that we had no reason to be proud of the heritage of privation and fear we bequeathed to the young. But we were naturally somewhat resentful when we were bluntly informed by our students that we had failed in our responsibilities to them, although we could not deny that there was some truth in the indictment. And, when we were told that our accepted values were worthless we were alarmed and disturbed. We were worried when it was asserted that liberalism, which we felt to be the most efficient vehicle of social progress, was out of date and that the time had come to apply more revolutionary tactics in the struggle for the reform of the social order. To some young men the methods of communism, with its self-righteous talk about ultimate democracy, seemed to have a disturbing attraction. Others frankly said they preferred the economic accomplishments of fascism to the free air of vacillating democracy.

In the economic field, the sudden transition from prosperity to severe depression was reflected in youth's demand for security, about which much was heard a decade ago. Because of a longer perspective, we who were older were more able to understand how unsubstantial the boom years of the 'twenties had been; but we forgot that for youth of the early 'thirties they were the only standard of comparison. To many of us in middle life, the fact that security should loom so large in the ambition of youth was disturbing.

As the clouds of war grew darker, we oldsters were further troubled by youth's loudly proclaimed doctrines of pacifism. We disliked being told that the last war had been fought for low and selfish motives because we knew that was not so. We feared that young men had become so indoctrinated by the cynicism of a few popular writers as to be blinded to the grave issues building up into a war that, we sensed, would strain the very foundations of our civilization. We failed to make due allowance for the fact that they were exercising their right to think for themselves, something we had always exhorted them to do. We forgot all this, and we neglected to remember how sensitive young men are to what is going on about them—and that when they start to think for themselves they always cause pain to their elders.

The imminent approach of war brought clarification. The fog of cynicism rolled back as young men by the hundreds of thousands entered the services of their country, and freely offered themselves to sustain those same values to which they seemed indifferent a few years ago. We are happy today in the realization that earlier fears were groundless, for we see those who had scorned patriotism as a doubtful virtue now demonstrating by deeds of unsurpassed courage that they cherish their country's ideals. Indeed, they seem to understand, often more clearly than many of their elders, that an inhuman evil force must be conquered by force if it is not to destroy what we esteem.

Former impatience with the weaknesses of democracy evaporates in a new comprehension that political and intellectual freedom is more to be regarded than the charms of a blueprint of a regimented social order. Contrasted with the grim insecurity of war, the economic security with which so many were concerned a few years ago seems but a trifle. Our young men are making good, and the decade that opened with criticism of their moral indifference closes with pride in their courage and fidelity.

Having thus resolved for themselves the grave issues that have marked the period of crisis into which they were thrust by the accident of birth, and having demonstrated that they can meet with fortitude the responsibilities involved in the defense of civilization against barbarism, how will our young men treat the opportunity and the responsibility that will be theirs when victory is won?

In a common military danger we are finding a new unity and a refreshed spirit of cooperation among all people. From this we may take courage. But let us be warned that all moments of danger induce social cohesion. For we know by experience that unity caused by pressure of war may turn out to be only momentary and may evaporate when the danger has passed. We need constantly to remember, what is becoming dangerously trite as a phrase, that winning the war will not of itself win the peace. Are we certain that when victory has been achieved, we shall as a nation be able to profit from the lessons of the war? Victory will not guarantee us against a relapse into those conditions which will breed new wars; it will only clear the stage for another chance. The danger that we shall revert is very great. We shall come out of the war fatigued in body and spirit, strongly tempted to prefer short-sighted palliatives to the intellectual labor of building new international relationships which alone promise a peaceful future.

It is the generation which is bearing the brunt of combat which will have to see to it that the lesson of this war will not be lost. When they return victorious and rich in honor, they must not indulge in the luxury of a moral slump, because they will have completed their job only in part. The American way of life cannot withstand more wars of the exhausting sweep and savagery which expanding technology will make possible. The next war will surpass the present one in destruction and death, as it in turn is exceeding the last. And so on ad infinitum, unless we are able to introduce the reign of law into international relationships.

The simple truth is that unless we organize for peace we shall not have peace. Unless the idea of international collaboration, which few dispute, *is incorporated in some political institution* it will remain a polite platitude. A political institution is an instrument of order and a means of making an idea effective. An institution is to an idea what the body is to the spirit of man. Without a political organization of nations to implement the sentiment of men for collaboration, we shall never prevent wars.

It is true that institutions cannot be created overnight; they are rooted in the past and they contain both rational and non-rational elements. But while these considerations impose limitations on the power of logic to change the political habits and attitudes of peoples, they do not destroy the role that conscious design and adaptation can play in human affairs. If we will it hard enough, we can now take the first steps toward an international order adequate to meet our most pressing dangers today and to provide a basis for peaceful growth in years to come.

No nation can hope to become strong enough in the post-war world to guarantee its own peace against all comers by its own power alone. Those who talk about a seven-ocean navy and a military force big enough for us to stand alone in a world of armed nations are muttering folly. The alternative to some sort of supranational organization is relapse into dependence on balance of power. Yet this alternative I conceive to be illusory. I know that there are those who believe sincerely in it as the best method of securing peace. And I concede that a delicate balance of power may have discouraged sporadic wars in the past. But it has always broken down in the end. Today's world is not the world of the nineteenth century, and any balance that might be achieved after this war would be too unstable to deserve the name. Science and technology have seen to that.

It is clear that any supranational organization which is to succeed must begin modestly. It must respect the emotional strength of existing national loyalties and outlooks. It must not attempt to frame a supergovernment so all-embracing and unfamiliar that man will not be prepared emotionally to participate in it, for obviously men's emotions, as well as their intellects, must be favorable to it. At the outset, therefore, it must be one of limited scope and simple in operation, directed to those areas in which world interdependence is strongest and in which international friction is most readily generated. We shall not succeed if we attempt too much. We shall likewise fail if we attempt too little.

All experienced students of international relations know that the obstacles which will have to be surmounted to attain any form of effective organized collaboration are exceedingly grave and formidable. These obstacles are increased rather than diminished when the structure and scope of the international organization which is proposed are too elaborate or too broad. This is not the moment to expound one's own thoughts as to the proper framework and functions of an attainable supranational government. Personally I should warn against excessive trust in political gadgets or mechanisms as such. The form of government is not the cause of good government but merely a means, although a necessary one, of effectuating the will of the people. Comprehensive schemes for world government may appear superficially logical but if they ignore history and human nature, they are doomed before they start. It would not be necessary to repeat this obvious truth were it not for the fact that it is so generally forgotten. Nevertheless, unless the desire for peace through the reign of law is incorporated in an international political organization, it will not prevail. I am not suggesting an over-elaborate organization at the start. All that is practicable at first is one that will function in those few, familiar areas in which the needs are greatest and most generally recognized. In this way I believe that we can achieve the reign of law in international trade, we can assure access to the raw materials of the earth on an equitable basis, and we can reduce the fear of insecurity and encirclement which is so often the psychological basis of war.

First, of course, we of the United Nations must accomplish the complete military defeat of our enemies. Only by being beaten into unconditional surrender will they learn that their long tradition of aggrandizement by force is evil and unprofitable. But we need not discuss this point further. Our men in the armed forces will attend to that.

When they return to ways of peace, our college graduates, I trust, will be prepared for heavier civic responsibilities than have been customary in the past. Democracy will be on trial then as always; the strain of reconstruction may test it as never before in our history. It cannot survive in a world of nations primed for war. Unless we can lay the specter of new and more terrible wars in the future, we shall not be able to establish an environment friendly to the solution of domestic problems or to realize our full possibilities for economic prosperity and human advancement. If at the end of this war we have to begin to prepare for the next; if we must continue to divert a large proportion of our national wealth and energy to war purposes; if we must militarize our national behavior to assure military security, we shall defeat the way of life we are now fighting to preserve. Those who will win this war in their own sweat and blood can see to it that this does not occur.

☆ ☆ ☆ ☆

IV. THE ANATOMY OF COURAGE

AT A TIME like this when the techniques of fear have become national instruments of destruction, all of us should understand the nature of fear and anxiety if we are to remain free to act wisely and competently.

Fear is a natural human emotion. In its rightful place it is beneficial. In proper proportion, fear compels us to weigh the consequences of our conduct and thus makes us wiser and more temperate human beings. Fear also may inspire to deeds of great courage and self-sacrifice. It may be the necessary call to action which awakens us from indolence or indifference when action is required. Thus by its restraining influence at one moment and by its driving power at another the emotion of fear works for self-preservation and self-realization.

But like most useful things in life, fear must be controlled or it will work harm rather than good. Instead of tempering our conduct when it should be tempered, it may drive us to rashness and folly; and instead of arousing a desire to act when action is needful it may work in the opposite direction by weakening or degrading the will. The rational man is not the one who never feels fear, but the one who refuses to be dominated by it.

The danger to which all of us, young and old, are exposed today, when there are so many reasons to be afraid, is that we shall become anxious. Anxiety is fear in a corrupted form. It is a sort of chronic fear. An anxious mind is one weakened by worries which color the whole life of the individual although he may not be aware of the cause. When one feels fear in its usual sense one is conscious of an objective danger which is rational and of which one would naturally be afraid, but when one is possessed by anxiety the fear is hidden and subjective and corrosive. It is a state of mind which few of us escape in some form and into which any of us may fall at any time. The average person does not understand the part that it plays in our lives. Anxiety may be one's chief obstacle to happiness and success, I repeat, without one being conscious of it.

As William James once said, "men habitually use only a small part of the powers which they possess and which they might use under appropriate circumstances." One reason for this is the presence of anxieties which lower our mental tone, dilute the will and condemn us to careers far below that which we should otherwise enjoy.

What can one do to prevent anxiety?

First, let us consider some methods which are often tried but which never succeed. We may seek to stupefy our anxieties with alcohol, narcotics, feverish social activities or frenzied overwork to the point of exhaustion. Not only are such efforts bound to fail, but they impair the function of the mind in the process. Another method is to pretend to ourselves that everything is all right when our reason tells us that it is not. Thus we are led to shun action when we should be active or to evade danger when we should run forward to meet it.

But as nature has made us subject to fears and anxieties so has she equipped us with valid means to resist and overcome them. The antidote to fear is courage. As Barrie said in his address as Rector of St. Andrews University "when courage goes everything goes," for, Dr. Johnson declares, "unless a man have that virtue he has no security for preserving any other."

How, then, can we build courage into our lives? How can we meet the threat of anxiety in the days ahead and thus be free to use our full latent powers as individuals and as a nation? Platitudes commanding us to be courageous are not very helpful in pointing out how we may cultivate courage. Something more is needed.

The solution is through self-knowledge. Although self-knowledge is by far the most difficult lesson of life, nowhere does the precept "Know Thyself" apply with greater force than here. And to self-knowledge we must add the stern discipline of self-control in applying the truths that self-knowledge teaches.

The first step is to understand that fear is as natural and universal as hunger. No rational person escapes it. There is no thoughtful person, no conscientious leader great or small, who does not experience it time and again. Boswell records an anecdote related by a friend of Dr. Johnson regarding the Emperor Charles V, who, when he read on the tombstone of a Spanish nobleman, "Here lies one who never knew fear," dryly remarked, "Then he never snuffed a candle with his fingers." In times of stress and danger, when one's fears can so easily become chronic anxieties, it helps to remember this.

The next step is to learn to recognize the symptoms of fear and anxiety in ourselves. Then one can, as it were, isolate the germ of his trouble and treat it as such. When one acknowledges that he is afraid; when one no longer strives to repress or conceal his fears from himself but frankly draws them into the full sunlight of his consciousness their power begins to wane. When one can feel fear and not be afraid he has developed courage. This I say in all humility, as one who does not pretend to be a courageous man but who has been helped by this technique in times of anxiety and who commends it as one aid to a good life.

In the last analysis, however, it is necessary to realize that the ultimate fountain of courage is not to be found in the applied psychology which I have been discussing. It is to be discovered rather in one's inner resources culminating in a belief in the spiritual ordering of the universe and an unshaken confidence in the final good no matter how strong the immediate evil. Whatever place one may assign to Martin Luther in world history, we can all admit that he had reasons to be afraid; yet from the depth of his own experience he assures us in his immortal hymn:

> A mighty Fortress is our God
> A Bulwark never failing.

The man who accepts these words and who makes them his own has established resources of the spirit against which anxiety cannot prevail. Those brave figures of the past who felt themselves to be in harmony with the will of the Almighty knew also that they were in communication with the Author of that moral courage which banishes fear. The prophets of the Old Testament foretold dire suffering and destruction for their nations, such as today we might describe as the end of civilization, yet they retained their faith in the victory of good over evil if men would but seek righteousness, and they were sustained thereby.

Now I realize that a sense of moral security such as this involves an act of faith and that there are some who prefer to place their trust in science where results, they may say, can be proved. Personally I do not believe that the findings of science can be proved in the broad sense in which the word is generally and loosely used, or indeed in any manner that will define the nature and destiny of man. But waiving the question as to whether or not the facts of science are susceptible of proof, the important point is that those familiar doctrines which set our ideals of daily life are acts of faith—not laws of science. If you believe in the integrity of the individual, if you cherish the values of democracy, if you favor a free society rather than one of vested privilege or tyranny, you do so by an act of faith. The basic principles of ethics to which we, consciously or unconsciously, pay allegiance were not derived from a study of anthropology, psychology, politics or economics. Rather are they a matter of faith which antedates the scientific methods of these scholarly subjects, and they still set the frame of reference for philosophy and the social studies. And they stem from the roots of the Christian faith.

And so I think that it is both rational and reasonable to acknowledge a power outside ourselves, a Divine Person of infinite goodness whose ways are not the ways of man but in whose being we can find refuge from anxieties which would oppress us.

I think it was this curse of anxiety which our Lord had in mind when, in the Sermon on the Mount, he told his disciples not to be anxious about the things of tomorrow but to seek first the Kingdom of God and His righteousness. It is as simple as that. It requires no theological embellishment. It is a mystery, but so is the sunrise.

☆ ☆ ☆ ☆ ☆

V. FREEDOM *AND* RESPONSIBILITY

In the year 1775, believing a war with England inevitable, a man who had failed twice in business and once as a farmer before he turned to the successful practice of the law and became a leader in propaganda for the independence of the Colonies, made a speech in the second revolutionary convention of Virginia which concluded with these words: "I know not what course others may take, but as for me, give me liberty or give me death." By this famous peroration Patrick Henry won immortality in the school history books and struck a responsive chord in the hearts of Americans which has not yet ceased to vibrate.

To our colonial forefathers the chief threat to liberty was government. Liberty, as they viewed it, was the absence of arbitrary civil restraints upon the self-realization of the individual. Destroy unnatural hindrances to the free play of natural reason imposed by arbitrary authority and all would be well.

We now know that this expectation was not realized. Hindsight being better than foresight, we are now able to realize that governmental tyranny is not the sole threat to our liberties. But let us not forget that underlying all other freedoms is civil freedom, and that our ancestors were correct in the importance they attached to it. Those who press for the all-embracing state—the utopia of bureaucrats—will do well to consider more seriously the loss of political liberty which they so lightly esteem. As one looks about the world, he can as an American be thankful to those heroic figures of past times who through the centuries struggled to establish the great liberties which we have come to accept casually as if they had existed forever.

A certain radical school of writers asserts that historically the demand for political liberty has been nothing more than the rationalization of a desire for a greater share of the property or privileges possessed by the few but withheld from the many. Thus the historic contests for freedom of government, of opinion, of speech, of assembly, of religious worship, are said to have been merely deceptive cloaks concealing the acquisitive urge to make money.

I submit that this is too low an appraisal of human nature. Our own war of independence had its economic aspects, to be sure, but of greater significance was its ideology which ran to the natural rights of individuals as human beings. No, man's quest for freedom cannot be explained in economic terms. When the Scottish Parliament in the time of Robert Bruce issued their manifesto against submission to English rule, it was not a regard for economic interest that moved them to declare: "It is liberty alone that we fight and contend for, which no honest man will lose but with his life." A few years ago, in our more enlightened age, some would have called this war-mongering, but millions are at this very moment matching it with their lives.

Our forefathers believed that love of liberty was a dominant native constituent of all human beings. Of late, however, we have seen in the Axis Nations that the sentiment for freedom can be bought off; that other sentiments may displace it; that man can be led into a willing surrender of his liberties. This leads us to a consideration of a distorted theory of freedom diametrically opposed to America's tradition but productive of sweeping and horrible consequences. To the German philosophers of the nineteenth century obsessed with the idea of order, the theories of freedom which underlay our War of Independence seemed to spell anarchy and disorder. Their temperamental fear of disunion made them hostile to liberty as understood in England and the United States, and led them to stress order imposed from above as the basic element necessary to cement society together.

Now it is true that order is required to sustain liberty. This is often difficult for young people to understand, as any college dean will testify. But the definition of freedom coined by the German philosophers is so extreme, so opposed to our own tradition that it is difficult for us to comprehend it. According to their doctrines, the highest freedom is found in the ordered life dictated by the rulers of the state. The individual is free to the extent that his life is dissolved in the state. True freedom is defined as submission, surely a twisted use of a good word. According to this concept, the ants and bees would appear to be freest of all living things.

I do not ask you to understand this doctrine which has for several generations characterized German thought. And yet we cannot deny its fearful power once it has become the ideal of a nation.

I have set forth these two antithetical doctrines of liberty, the one which stresses the individual's right to a life of his own and the other the individual's subjection to the state, for a very specific purpose, viz., to point out one characteristic which they have in common. Although poles apart in other respects, each has a common element without which any theory of freedom would be nonsense. It is recognition of the truth that liberty for each individual implies a harmonious relationship to a force or power outside and above himself to which he is, in the last analysis, accountable. In other words, no philosophy of liberty can escape the stern fact of responsibility.

Thus, the most extreme doctrines of individual liberty ever current in America insisted upon man's duty to obey reason. No man or nation declining this responsibility could be free. To the sorrow of our rationalistic forefathers the goddess of reason failed to establish dominion over the minds of men, as it was expected she would, but this did not alter the principle that liberty, in the old phrase, is not license to act capriciously. All free action is integrated action.

For example, we speak of a free golf swing. But a golf swing is free only when it is under control, when it is in tune with the forces upon which it depends. Similarly a free person is one in tune with his own being and with the powers to which he is accountable. No person who is not free in this sense is able to express himself to the full.

Assuming as I do that the fullest freedom is desirable, what is that ultimate force or power with which we must be in tune in order that we may be free, in order that we may live satisfying and purposeful lives? To what shall we render accountability? As the thoughtful person looks about today he discovers that in America the answers to this eternal question group themselves into two chief contending schools of thought. One school invokes the infallibility of an all-embracing science as the power which should command our exclusive allegiance. Entrust our harried lives to science and it will set us free; it is our only hope. The second school denies such absolutism to science and declares that man's most controlling responsibilities and possibilities are revealed only in the age-old religious aspirations of the human heart.

Let us consider first the case for science. Our imagination is unable to chart the future promise which science holds for human happiness. Advancing knowledge supplied by science has swept away (and will continue to sweep away) many beliefs regarding man which cramped and enslaved his spirit in the past. No longer is an epidemic or tornado viewed as an act of divine punishment. We owe an immeasurable debt to Hippocrates for the scientific principle that disease is nature and not spirits. Another debt is due Galileo for insisting that truth about the natural world can be gained more readily by observation of phenomena than by echoing Aristotle. Bacon has written that "knowledge and human power are synonymous" and we may confidently assume that the forward march of science will aid, not only by adding to our power to realize human ends but also by elevating and refining such ends. This I believe to be so despite the common observation that as yet science has done more to place new and more efficient tools at the disposition of our lower instincts than of our higher. If this be true, human depravity and not science has been to blame.

But we may acclaim the findings and methods of science and still deny that it carries with it a totalitarian mandate. Those who urge science as a substitute for the Deity talk in mysteries as obscure as any religionist ever employed. To them, science is the new religion, so our decision really boils down to this: What religion shall we accept?

Furthermore, those who would replace the Christian religion with the imperial claims of science often exhibit one characteristic which is commonly overlooked. This is a tendency toward a distrust of democracy and an intellectual aloofness from the needs and aspirations of the common man. For the democratically chosen leader, many of this group would substitute the scientific expert who is to become literally the messiah of a new age.

It is when they describe the all-powerful part to be played by the expert in a world worshipping at the feet of science that they let the cat out of the bag. We are told that modern life has become so intricate and unintelligible to the common man that he cannot longer be expected to possess a helpful opinion regarding his own welfare or the means of bringing it about. Society must, therefore, submit to the skill and disinterestedness of the scientist employed in the service of the state rather than trust in democratically formed public opinion. When society agrees to rely on the expert, it is said, it will have begun to develop a brain. Now democracy needs experts, and ours can be criticized for the slight use it has made of them, but the common man's unwillingness to accept the tyranny of the scientist is natural and correct. Life controlled in the name of science by a few experts to whom the common man is to entrust his destiny runs counter not only to the best social science, but to democratic fundamentals as well. Who will choose the experts? What will happen if they cannot agree among themselves or if they develop strange ideas about basic human needs? What will happen to the liberty and dignity of the common man when he is persuaded that it is better that he permit the expert to define his needs and fix his ends for him? No, scientific absolutism is to be rejected if only for the reason that it would set up a new priesthood whose rule would be in fact the rule of the vested interests and the vested ideas of a class of co-opted scientists.

Let us turn now to the other school of thought regarding the source of power to set men free. Christianity insists that "personality is the great central fact of the universe." It acknowledges man's capacity and craving for fellowship with a supernatural and eternal personality, and asserts that only in such fellowship will our spirits find a final explanation of and satisfaction for our highest desires. God cannot be proved by the methods of science any more than the existence of truth and beauty can be proved. But in the words of one eminent scientist "the hypothesis of God gives a more reasonable interpretation of the world than any other." Any man, I may add, can be proud to make this interpretation his own. All history proves, said Professor Shorey, the truth of Homer's statement that all men have need of God. Lord Tweedsmuir in his posthumous autobiography tells us that he wanted no philosophy to rationalize the fundamentals of the Christian religion, for they seemed to him so completely rational.

The right to freedom must be earned anew every day, and it is by meeting our responsibilities that we attain unto it. Many dread liberty, as Bernard Shaw said, because it means responsibility. Freedom is made of stern stuff and not a few break down in their effort to qualify for it. If we refuse the rigors of self-discipline we are doomed to fall into slavery.

For a decade or more the world has lived in bondage to fear. Why have the peoples been afraid? Is it not in large measure because of a widespread renunciation of responsibilities? We have seen nations, statesmen and individuals deny most solemn obligations even when established in binding contractual form, and in so doing they have wounded liberty. But it has not been destroyed in the hearts of men and it will be restored to its place of power when the world is again willing to accept its conditions.

☆ ☆ ☆ ☆ ☆ ☆

VI. THE CASE FOR LIBERALISM

A CLASS valedictorian recently did me the honor to refer to the general political philosophy that commands my allegiance as "old-fashioned liberalism," a label which, I must confess, I had used in his hearing and around which he threw humorous and kindly quotation marks.

In my day in college, liberalism was the dominant philosophy of progressives. Can it be true, I asked myself, that a faith which for many decades exercised such influence over the thought of man and which displayed such survival and adaptive power is now outworn and obsolete? Or is it rather that the meaning of that faith is not fully understood by recent college generations who have heard most about it from its enemies; and may it not be true that a better knowledge of what liberalism stands for will lead to a renewed respect for it?

It is true that large numbers of people throughout the world have repudiated liberalism as outmoded and sterile. What is needed, they contend, is something more virile, more positive, more self-assured. There is much injustice in the world and many heads to be broken. Let us hasten, they say, to our appointed tasks which our fathers were too complacent to recognize or too timid to perform.

Unfortunately for its own good, liberalism is a word used vaguely by thousands who little understand what it signifies. Let us define it, then describe its past accomplishments and future possibilities, and finally place in contrast to it its most ardent philosophical competitor.

In the first place, liberalism, as I am using the term, does not refer to the platform of any political party by whatever name it may be called. It is a faith regarding the individual and society which has influenced all political parties from time to time in greater or less degree. It is more fundamental than party politics.

Neither do I refer to any specific school of theology. Liberalism is a way of life, a habit of mind. In essence it is "the disposition of the man who looks upon each of his fellows as of equal worth with himself." It emphasizes the value of the human spirit. Liberalism stands for the emancipation of persons and groups from external conditions which hamper and degrade the free play of personality. It is opposed to regimentation. It would use the power of the state to remove obstacles to freedom rather than to enforce patterns of economic or social behavior. It insists that difficult questions are settled better by discussion than by force. Let those who would condemn it to obsolescence remember that it is only in those countries which are still under its sway that a man may with safety assert his own opinions, and there he may do so even if such opinions advocate the destruction of the freedom which permits him to express his views.

Let us admit at the start that liberalism offers no cut and dried cure-all for human ills. Believing that society is composed of living persons and not automata, it makes no pretensions to cocksure revolutionary programs. If this be weakness, make the most of it. To me it is obvious common sense.

I have intimated that the enemies of liberalism dismiss it as a negative doctrine and insist that something more positive is required. It is true that in its infancy liberalism had much in common with *laissez faire*, but it is incorrect to bracket the two today. In the eighteenth century the world was ruled by laws and customs which favored the few and hindered by artificial restrictions the freedom and opportunities of the many. The first duty of reform was, therefore, to destroy the regimentation of the society of the day. For one hundred years liberalism worked to abolish arbitrary government in favor of popular government and universal suffrage. It rebelled against inherited class privileges which excluded large elements of the population from opportunities for an education and a career. It struck at monopolies, legalized and sustained by the state, which suppressed the free enterprise of the average man. It struggled successfully against ecclesiastical and political domination of opinion. It established the right of labor to organize in its own behalf and the right of newspapers to criticize the government. It promoted the equality of the sexes and denied that caste systems were a proper pattern for society. These are no mean accomplishments. Although negative in the sense that they were directed at the removal of excrescences, they nevertheless aggregate a magnificent total of constructive gains.

In view of the withering hand which government once held upon the ambitions of the common man, it was but natural that the socially-conscious liberal of the time should have sought to reduce the functions of government and should have exaggerated the opportunity for the free play of natural capacities which would flow from a reduction of governmental interference in the lives of people. Yet early liberalism is not to be despised on this account. Social advance required that artificial hindrances be removed. If the negative side of liberalism was dominant in its youthful stages, its work of destruction was necessary to prepare the way for more affirmative action later.

With the flowering of the industrial revolution new forms of human bondage appeared of which earlier liberals had not been aware. The suffering produced by the new and crude factory system, the virtual enslavement of laborers, the exploitation of women and children, the squalor and disease which characterized the transition from a domestic to an industrial economy, spelled oppression of individuals as truly as had the earlier forms of selfish power against which the liberals first inveighed. The time had come for liberalism to transfer its attention from the removal of discriminatory governmental restrictions to positive measures to establish social conditions in which the citizen would not again be estopped from developing his innate opportunities.

Liberals therefore have not feared to use the affirmative power of the state, as the chief instrument of social regulation, to prevent the concentration and abuse of private powers which tend to accumulate in any society. Consequently the past two generations have seen a great expansion of the scope of government.

Many undertakings once considered the private business of the individual are now regulated in considerable detail. The interests of workers are safeguarded by hundreds of statutes and administrative orders. Public education consumes what once would have been the wealth of an empire. In a hundred directions the service activities of government seek to hold out a helping hand. While these operations of government have frequently been called socialistic, the dominant spirit behind them has never been socialistic in any accurate sense. The genius of America has not been collectivistic.

I am not arguing that these newer activities of government have always been wise, efficient, or even honest. What I am arguing for is a point of view, a social philosophy which endorses every measure which will free individuals from social and economic handicaps, but which tests every proposal by its probable effect upon individuals and not by some romantic conception of the nation or society. As the liberal state differs from the autocratic, antisocial state against which it reacted one hundred and fifty years ago, so it must differ from any form of social organization which replaces individual responsibility by a state responsibility into which the individual is to be absorbed.

While the humility of liberalism renders a man cautious in interfering in the development of others, its human sympathies nevertheless lead to active, positive steps to remove barriers to the development of personality. Like Christianity it has always had to struggle for recognition in the lives of men and nations. It has colored all western thought, but like Christianity its sway over human conduct has ever been partial and intermittent. But its victories, measured in a progressive diffusion of well-being throughout the years, have been sufficient to suggest that, although as a guide to public policy it is the least pretentious, it is the most promising.

This truth becomes clear when we examine liberalism's chief philosophical antagonist, dialectical materialism. This impressive phrase is the label usually applied to the philosophy of Karl Marx which, either in its crude shape or in the form of numerous derivations, claims to have discovered economic laws which operate blindly upon the lives of men, which can be formulated in scientific terms, and which dictate how the spirit of man will express itself, if indeed it will concede that man has a spirit.

Most educated people have at least a speaking acquaintance with Marx's economic theory. But Marx's philosophy of dialectical materialism, by which he sought to integrate his economic concepts, is mysterious, difficult to understand and explain, and still more difficult to accept. His view is that the great world process, the continuous activating principle in human life, is not spiritual but economic: Religious beliefs, moral standards and political ideas are but a reflection of the prevailing system of production and distribution of goods. Man cannot improve his nature by the force of ideals because it is the material world alone that fixes the forms which his ideals may take. Being the creature of the economic system of the moment, his only hope for a better life is from changes in that system.

Marx and his followers claim that this naïve doctrine of human perfectibility has a scientific basis and that future developments can be predicted with scientific accuracy. But to call it scientific adds no validity to a theory which admits of no scientific tests and follows no scientific methodology. No scientist has yet formulated social laws which have met the test of time as reliable bases of prediction. To claim the authority of the word "scientific" for communism is to misuse a good word for the sake of the prestige it carries.

The urge to be scientific has frequently misled scholars seeking a single principle to explain social phenomena, and Marx was no exception. Scholars, writes Mr. Robert B. Lloyd, are apt to define civilization in terms of society; the plain man will do so in terms of personality. In this case, as frequently happens, the plain man is right. To me dialectical materialism is but an extreme example of mystical and wishful thinking.

The followers of Marxism advocate the dictatorship of the proletariat, but it is often not realized that they do not mean so much dictatorship *by* the proletariat as dictatorship *over* the proletariat. They believe that free and democratic government is at best a distant possibility. They assert the necessity and right of authoritarian rule by the small intelligent minority who, regardless of the consent of the governed, must guide the incompetent majority. By a bold plunge into obscure mysteries which I cannot comprehend, they promise that the use of power by the small leader class will not be distorted by selfish interests.

That, under communism, irresponsible power will be exercised in the public interest is merely an improbable assertion which all experience denies. When self-selected individuals, no matter how virtuous they think themselves to be, claim the power of life and death over others because of their superior capacity or the purity of their motives, they are indeed to be feared. For as Santayana has said, a zeal sufficient to destroy selfishness may, by turning virtue into fanaticism, be worse than selfishness.

Liberalism rejects dialectical materialism as a philosophy and scorns its practical program of revolution, terror and dictatorship. The liberal denies that a method in itself reprehensible and inconsistent with the goal to be attained can ever accomplish a morally acceptable purpose. Immoral means do not give beneficent results. Self-corrosion sets in and nullifies the attempt. History is too rich in disastrous examples of efforts by zealous and even altruistic people to exercise peculiar and absolute power over others to convince one that possession of irresponsible power can remain beneficent, no matter how high-sounding and sincere are the allegations of those vested with it.

This issue between dialectical materialism and liberalism is the modern version of the age-old contest of the body versus the spirit. Because of the very limitations which it imposes upon itself science can provide no answer. The part of wisdom is to understand that man's ultimate destiny is personal and spiritual and to ignore any pseudo-scientific explanation which rests upon the analogy of natural forces with which true science deals. The liberal believes that "history is a spiritual achievement," not merely the reflected image of an economic order. The ethic of liberalism is the Christian ethic.

☆ ☆ ☆ ☆ ☆ ☆ ☆

VII. "HE THAT'S SECURE IS NOT SAFE"*

THIS eighteenth-century adage has a hollow ring for the modern man, intent upon building defenses against the insecurities of life which our large-scale economy has developed. And yet security, like certain other blessings, has a way of eluding those who pursue it most assiduously. As an antidote to modern preoccupation with personal security, Benjamin Franklin's advice is worthy of careful re-appraisal, particularly by young men for whom life can still be an adventure with higher stakes than mere avoidance of risks.

Of course life has always been insecure, but of late insecurity has taken new and strange forms. In pioneer days the struggle was more concerned with the errant forces of nature, unpredictable in their cruelty yet familiar in their manifestations and therefore less terrifying than the hidden snares of insecurity today. Today the insecurity of which millions are so conscious seems to be the consequence of human folly and perversity, in that it springs from man's struggle with man rather than from the age-old familiar struggle with nature. The paradox of the hour is man's universal confidence in himself in respect to technology and science and his gnawing feeling of insecurity in respect to his relations with others, colored by a profound skepticism as to his capacity to resolve his self-made difficulties.

* This is the substance of the Baccalaureate Address to the Princeton Class of 1937. It was directed against a misplaced emphasis on economic security, which was prevailing at the time and which had begun to infect the minds of college students. It is not a criticism of "collective" security in international relations or of "job" or "social" security in the sense that the fear of want must be reduced if that minimum degree of security necessary to release incentive is to prevail. The address is included here because it will be relevant after the war to young people of the sort to whom it was directed before the war. The importance of work and the need for job security are discussed in the next chapter.

Under these circumstances, it is not surprising that the world should be grasping at numerous and contradictory formulas for attaining security to the point that in our quest for happiness we are in danger of elevating security from the minor position in which it belongs to a dominant place in the scale of human values. Once our society does that, no one can predict what follies will be committed in the name of humanity. That their positive effect will be to throw out the baby with the bath is, however, predictable.

To suggest that the emphasis on security may not only retard progress but actually militate against the attainment of security itself, is not to be forgetful of the suffering which economic insecurity brings to large elements of our population. The fear of unemployment, from which masses of our fellow citizens even in good times are never exempt, need not be experienced to enable one to understand that security against abject need is essential if we are to be a nation of free men. Men and women are truly free only when their bodies are free from dehumanizing want and their minds free from external domination which the fear of want entails. And only a free people can be a democratic people. Indeed the instinct for security is so strong among the mass of mankind that they will readily yield freedom rather than be condemned to a craven insecurity. Only when we have grasped this fact are we able to understand the grip which dictatorship can exert upon the loyalties of a people and realize why the precious jewel of freedom may so willingly be bartered away. But the point which I am seeking to expound is that, by confining its eyes to the limited horizon of security, a nation may not only wither its own soul but may act positively to defeat the economic as well as the spiritual security which it seeks. Preoccupation with security breeds insecurity.

World War I left among nations a heritage of fear as devastating as hate. Before such fears, many previously accepted spiritual and humanitarian values went down to temporary defeat. In nation after nation we find that even the normal peacetime activities of government had been organized on a basis of internal war, with the spirit and emotion of war characterizing all domestic activities as a means to internal, as well as external, security. It is not necessary to argue that when the spirit of militarism and exaltation of dictatorship pervade the life of a people the future of that people is thereby made insecure.

In the field of international organization we find that to military armaments were added the burden of economic armaments, tariffs, embargoes, bounties, quotas and preferences, employed for the same purpose which military force is designed to serve. The ultimate cost of these vain instruments of security in terms of economic distress and human suffering cannot be estimated statistically, but unless other motives can be substituted after this war they will again be catastrophic in their consequences.

In our own country preoccupation with thoughts of security before Pearl Harbor led to the adoption of neutrality legislation doomed to fail when tested because, as is always the case when security becomes the dominating purpose, we found that in our eagerness to render ourselves secure we became merely the inert and unwitting victims of circumstance rather than its masters. The ostrich with its head in the sand is seeking security.

In the field of domestic economics similar self-defeating policies were proposed to cure economic ills. We were told that rapid scientific advancement creates problems of economic maladjustment faster than we are able to solve them. In the interests of stability and security a repressive policy toward new scientific discoveries and new technological processes was proposed. We were actually promised in some quarters that we should have more goods to enjoy if fewer goods were produced. True, the speed with which economic innovations have been introduced has involved friction. Unfortunately those who have had to suffer this friction most severely have often been the ones least able to bear it. But to reduce friction it is not necessary or wise to cease operating a productive machine. Our prosperity depends upon our learning to absorb and adapt innovations instead of rejecting them as harmful to peace and order. If history demonstrates anything it is that in a stagnant state of society we may expect under-employment and economic distress to be the rule rather than the exception. In our history the periods of fullest employment, of greatest exertion of productive power, have been periods of change.

The danger here, as always when one is engrossed in thoughts of security, is stagnation. "Art thou drowned in security? Then I say thou art perfectly dead," declared Francis Bacon. The price of progress is change; absence of change is death. Social engineering may be able to release us from the horrors of the business cycle, but when we make the mistake of placing our hope in measures of security rather than in a willingness to venture toward larger growth, decay has begun.

As I have already intimated, one strong appeal of the authoritarian state is its plausible promise of security without personal responsibility. Individuals, it is argued, make many errors in business and social judgment because they are unable to comprehend and control the variables, the "deuces wild," in a dynamic world. "But," says the totalitarian state, "where you as individuals have failed I can predict wisely; I am the all-inclusive spiritual personality endowed with the mysterious gift of omniscience. You have only to trust me."

To the objective observer the hope for security which this promise holds out is void. It is more realistic to expect that once the state has received great power it will use that power to mask its mistakes and to force people to act as it deems they should, in order that the promises of the state may come true. No authoritarian state can afford to make mistakes, or rather, no authoritarian state can afford to permit the people to know that it does make mistakes. Preferably will it resort to crude force and pagan philosophies to preserve its prestige, until at last the people realize that the security promised is no security and that for human beings liberty and freedom of growth are basic to everything.

For society, concentration upon security as a goal is suicidal, doomed to practical as well as spiritual failure. By the same token the individual who lives for security is also throttling his powers and starving his soul.

The span of our powers being so limited, it is my sober belief that young college people cannot afford in their journey through life to burden their luggage with thoughts of security. Like happiness, security at best is a by-product recovered in the process of living. Courage is a better motto than security and offers far brighter prospects of social stability and self-realization. The man who keeps his eye fixed on security inevitably becomes enmeshed in the tentacles of the status quo. Engrossed in such a narrow objective he loses his best chance for security.

It is an old adage that the way to be safe is never to be secure. I remember a comment by Professor Spaeth, who coached Princeton crews on Lake Carnegie for many years, in support of Benjamin Franklin's aphorism that he who is secure is not safe. It was his observation as a coach that the very moment at which a man began to think his place in the boat was assured was the moment at which it was by the very thought rendered unsafe. His puddles weren't as big as they were before, was the coach's way of expressing it.

One of the tragedies of life is the readiness with which a natural and proper attention to a reasonable measure of security in this world shades off into a craven occupation with considerations of material self-interest, forgetful of the security of the soul, in comparison with which worldly security is but dust and ashes in the mouth. The courage to venture material welfare in a materialistic age, to turn one's back upon ambitions of power or social position in favor of the unseen life of the spirit, to face the dangers of the moment in order that one may capture the certainty of the eternal, is the highest expression to which the ambition of man may aspire.

"Out of this nettle, danger," said Shakespeare, "we pluck this flower, safety." In even more eloquent words was the folly of any other philosophy expressed by our Lord in the brief, memorable phrase, "He that findeth his life shall lose it." May our days be lived with this grave warning ever present in our minds.

VIII. DEMOCRACY'S CHALLENGE TO PRIVATE AND COMMUNITY ENTERPRISE

It is generally agreed that the new government controls, national and international, over the production and distribution of goods introduced during the war, must not be relaxed too speedily afterwards. Undoubtedly many will survive the period of reconstruction and become an integral part of our political system. Unlike tidal waves, waves of expanding governmental power never recede to "normal." The United States has been under a crisis psychology for more than a decade. First it was economic depression, then war. As Sorokin truthfully points out in his recent book on *Man and Society in Calamity*, the main effect of calamities on the political structure of society is a marked expansion of governmental regulation, with corresponding decrease in freedom and decline of democratic and constitutional institutions. Political leaders in their quest for votes often try to cultivate a feeling of crisis to support their claims to office and power. This well known political strategy was quite familiar before the war. It is undoubtedly valid during the war, but we must guard against it afterwards. Our long-term peace policies should not be worked out in that mental state of uncritical dependence on government which crisis engenders.

That much that was done in the past decade will not be undone is demonstrated by the fact that the opposition political party has no serious intention of repealing the great bulk of the New Deal legislation. Whole areas of policy bitterly contested at the time of adoption are, as a practical political matter, now beyond controversy except as to details of application.

At the end of the war what government should do and what can best be left to private incentive and decision will be warmly debated all over the world. The answer in England and Europe promises to be more radical than in the United States. In other words, a larger element of traditional capitalism will be preserved with us than perhaps anywhere else in the world. Reports from England, for example, agree that the middle class heretofore relatively conservative in outlook, is moving more rapidly to left wing radicalism than the present political complexion of a Parliament that was elected eight years ago would suggest. And we can be sure that America will not return to the *status quo ante*; history never does.

If our economic life is not to be a discordant patchwork of various and variegated experiments, if there is to be system behind the programs of government and of business, it is essential that we develop a better national understanding of the sphere and nature of the state. One's view of the nature of government is apt to change with circumstances. If his business is experiencing new and vexatious governmental controls, the state to him is a surly policeman and little else. If, on the other hand, he is profiting from subsidies or other forms of tax-supported enterprises, the government resembles a kindly gentleman whose mission is to give pleasure to all. Neither view expresses the whole story, and it is important that we remember the whole story when we come to make up our minds as to how much or how little government we want. The fact is that government is something more than a policeman and less than a disinterested philanthropist. Since 1929 large numbers of voters have been apt to forget the brute-force side of the state while concentrating on its benevolence.

When one thinks about the function of government after the war he immediately becomes involved in the age-old problem of the part that force is to play in human affairs. The state is the sole agency with the moral right to use force to enforce its will. The state has a legal and moral monopoly on force. This sets it apart from all other forms of human association. It is force organized, and it tolerates no competition. In international affairs, its right to exert force is expressed ultimately in war; in domestic affairs its force culminates in its power of imprisonment and death. Therefore, each expansion of political power heightens the importance of adequate political controls, as the Constitutional fathers well knew. Because the force of the state is exercised not by supermen or angels, but by mere men who are forever subject to the intoxicating effects of power and to the temptation to use power for self-aggrandizement, it is to the interest of the average citizen that checks be placed on the power of the state and that government be always responsive to democratic controls. It is a commentary on our political thinking of the last ten years that the public has paid so little attention to the need of stronger political controls to match growing governmental power. Congress is no more efficient and adequately organized and staffed for this purpose than it was when the power of the executive was a mere embryo of its present magnitude.

By now most of us are fully aware of the role of force in international relations. Indeed we are fighting this war to refute the idea that one state can claim full freedom of action toward other states. But we are apt to lose sight of the fact that in its relations with its own citizens the state is likewise an organization of force. In the post-war days when the line of least resistance may be an uncritical expansion of the power of government over our daily lives, it will be well for us to remember that this expansion involves dangers more real than many well-intentioned people understand. If, because of an incomplete social idealism or because of a lazy choice of the easiest way out of our difficulties, we surrender to government functions which properly belong to private or community enterprise, the consequence may be the creation of concentrated political power more devastating than any consolidation of economic power this country has ever seen.

We shall have to be especially wary of the philosophy of those extreme social planners which promises the millennium in return for servitude to the state. Those who will say, "Just turn your worries over to us and we will see that you get more of the world's goods and relieve you of the burden of responsibility for yourself," are especially to be feared.

Of course, no "total social planner" in a democratic nation conceives of his program for state control as leading to full freedom of action by the state. But the truth is that the ultimate destination of the all-out planners is an all-inclusive state. When off guard, they reveal the inevitability of this trend by their impatience with existing political controls designed to preserve our political liberty, without which there can be no liberty of any kind. That the desire to be free of political controls may arise from the highest humanitarian motives to do good, as the official sees the good, does not alter the dangers of concentrated executive power. "Virtue itself has need of limits," said Montesquieu.

There are several reasons why we should be on guard against any philosophy tending to the acceptance of the all-inclusive state and its inescapable corollary, the moral claim to full freedom of action for the state.

1. *The All-Inclusive State would be autocratic and not democratic.* No official responsible for feeding a nation and directing its economic life could long afford to submit vital parts of his program to the risks of being upset by political opposition—nor could he pay much consideration to the rights of the minority to oppose and obstruct, respect for which is the essence of liberty. All political experience suggests that no mistakes would be publicly admitted; each one would be covered up by assertions of more power. The slogan of the all-inclusive state has been humorously expressed as "a chicken in every pot and a finger in every pie." It would need to have a finger in every pie if its schemes for a chicken in every pot were not to be disrupted by counter proposals of different ways to accomplish this desirable end.

2. *The All-Inclusive State would retard economic progress.* It would be monopolistic in its outlook and its policies would tend to restrictionism. The state plays the role of politician more naturally than that of a producer or enterpriser. Experience with the food problem in the United States and elsewhere reveals universal attempts to keep prices up by artificial scarcities—a conventional feature of all monopolies. And we have seen that when governments have experimented with the "un-normal growing" plan for agricultural control the ultimate considerations have been political rather than economic. In the long run the effort of

the all-inclusive state toward the business which it managed or controlled would be to maintain the status quo by preserving the marginal and the inefficient whose political strength would be considerable. For the same reason it would be reluctant to purge the economic system of obsolescence and waste. Economic progress comes by cheapening costs of goods and services through new methods and improvements. These are in turn the product of the "creative minority," which in any society must be relied on to blaze the trails of progress. Society cannot improve conditions for the common man unless it allows full opportunity for the uncommon man. The danger in "levelling" schemes lies in their failure to understand this.

Of course, the state is not the only agency that can stifle and repress the uncommon man. Big business, particularly when monopolistic in nature, may do the same. Indeed big business as well as government is subject to the weaknesses and inefficiency of bureaucracy.

3. *The All-Inclusive State would make for war rather than for peace.* Economic decisions and competition between one country and another would be moved from the realm of private decisions into the domain of grand strategy between states. Businessmen of one nation would no longer operate in personal competition with those of another. I do not mean to assert that governments today, even the most democratic, remain remote from involvements over the private business interests of their citizens. But the elimination of private business decisions and private intercourse between citizens of different states would be inevitable under collectivism. Under such circumstances all business negotiations across national boundaries would involve national prestige and honor, and this would make for war. All business life would be one state against another, with their armies and navies backing up their arguments.

If the case against the all-inclusive state is so strong why have we been moving, however reluctantly, more and more toward it in recent years? There are various reasons. Americans have been as ready as other people to turn to the state when the going becomes hard, and from one point of view the experience of the past depression was but a repetition of earlier ones in this respect. Other reasons, more difficult to appraise, relate to the gap that has appeared between the conditions of modern industrial life and the satisfaction of certain deep instincts which a more simple economy gratified more adequately. In other words, part of the drive toward state action springs from the frustration of powerful innate psychological urges. Two of these are the desire of each normal individual for a reasonable degree of economic security, and the desire to participate or to "belong."

While it is true that too much concern for security can thwart the higher energies of men and nations, it is also true that a minimum degree of security is basic to incentive.* The need for some degree of security to inspire the highest human aspirations was expressed in the Prayer Book of Elizabethan England in these words: "They that are snared and entangled in the utter lack of things needful for the body cannot set their minds upon Thee as they ought to do; but when they are deprived of things which they greatly desire, their hearts are cast down and quail for grief." Our forefathers were not secure as we count security today. The modern demand for security would have sounded strange to their ears. But it was the forces of nature with which they were contending—not man-made difficulties. The pioneers did not know the haunting fear of unemployment as thousands do today throughout every business cycle. There was work for them to do. None of them ever felt so helpless and unwanted as does a man out of a job in our modern industrial society. The only democratic solution for this problem is for business to balance the efforts of government by accepting social responsibilities for the cure of unemployment and for wider dispersion of the benefits of technological advance. If business follows the advice of some of its wisest representatives industrial leadership will by cooperative measures show the way to job security and higher

* In Chapter VII are discussed the dangers of over-emphasis on personal security.

standards of living. Thus it will remove by so much the reasons for state intervention.

The programs for full employment which are currently receiving most attention rely on public spending for the solution of our difficulties. The formula proposed is seductively simple and naturally attractive to legislators and public officials. Extraordinary public spending will be necessary undoubtedly for a period after the war but the danger is that it will become a habit. Although the spenders assert that private enterprise will have its place, public effort being applied only where private effort falls short, there is a disturbing overtone which suggests that the spenders expect private enterprise to fail. Indeed some seem to hope that it will. If I could feel that those who believe in the importance of private enterprise were constructively intent upon devising programs to make public spending unnecessary, and thus remove the temptation to passive reliance on it, I should be happier regarding the immediate outcome. "Security with freedom" is an excellent slogan but it will prove to be a contradiction in terms if private enterprise is excluded or if it disqualifies itself through inertia.

It will require all the common sense and all the social science we can muster to bring harmony to modern life at the economic level, but we shall be led into a trap if we forget that there are deeper elements to human frustration than material success or failure. Modern medicine and psychology reveal the error in all forms of materialism when they assert on the basis of clinical observations that the sense of emptiness and failure, the feeling of being stuck, may exist irrespective of economic circumstances.

Something more is necessary, therefore, in addition to a reasonable degree of job security. We must seek new ways and means, in our large-scale organization of life, to enable the average man to satisfy the urge to make his life count as an individual, to enjoy a sense of participation in constructive work, to have a feeling of being of some importance in the post he fills. If we are to preserve individualism there must be opportunity for individuals to participate as men and not as mere instruments of production.

Informed people view with grave concern the routine character of many a man's occupation which denies to him the personal satisfaction in his work which his forefathers enjoyed. The typical workman today, an employee and not an owner, and condemned too often to monotonous tasks, is beginning to look outside his job for the gratification of those creative impulses which every virile person possesses. Some tell us that such gratification can be found henceforth only in leisure-time opportunities, and that it is society's duty to supply them, else our thirst for self-expression will be slaked in violent and subversive measures. The assumption is that millions of us, so far as our jobs are concerned, are doomed to soul-destroying drudgery and that our real lives can be lived only in the leisure portion of our days. Under modern conditions, we are told, work is an evil to be reduced to the lowest possible minimum.

In this philosophy lurks a grave fallacy. The diagnosis is convincing but the treatment prescribed is not directed to the disease at all. The assumption that a man can express his real self in leisure-time activity and be happy in it contains a fundamental psychological error. Leisure is essential, but no matter how profitably employed it is no substitute for work. It is by demonstrating his worth as a worker, not by his prowess in recreation, that a man wins self-respect and the respect of others. Only through work does a man arrive at meaningful living. Those who ridicule what they derisively term "a feverish devotion to the goodness of work" forget that no amount of leisure is a substitute for purposeful work such as a man's true soul craves. Here is to be found one important explanation why fascism and communism, despite the patent evils of their philosophies, gave to their followers a new meaning of existence which transcends the humdrum tasks they are required to perform. In these tasks their work is related, however mistakenly, to a larger end outside themselves, and one which to them seems worth believing in and fighting for.

In the interest of social change by peaceful methods we should not blink the fact that countless numbers of people throughout the world are bound to jobs which, by depriving them of a sense of participation in a creative process, tend to starve their deeply ingrained work instincts. If one's work is such as to famish rather than to nourish one's craving to be a productive human being, it is to be expected that he will seek satisfaction elsewhere. May it not be that much of our economic and social unrest really stems from the truth that, for many, the working hours are a socially starved part of the day; that the forms which labor unrest takes may be but symptoms of a hidden discontent deeper than hours and wages—namely, the fact that the job does not provide an adequate work experience? The solution must be found in modifying the relationships under which men work. How to regain that richness of experience which our forefathers enjoyed when they were subduing a continent is a matter of concern to alert industrial leaders. It is the heart of the problem of industrial relations and personnel management. The subject requires for solution both good will and extensive scientific research.

This question of participation extends beyond the job to the community. Stability, mental peace, and lasting happiness can be found only in stable community relationships. The excessive mobility of population these days and the absence of natural neighborhood relationships constitute a menace because they do not satisfy the need of people for neighbors. You can live a long time in any city before you say "Good morning, neighbor." It used to be common when cities were smaller. There are too many lost individuals in a modern city. This is unnatural and dangerous. Small-town conversation around the old cracker barrel may have been trivial, but it satisfied the human desire for social participation for which urban life has as yet found no satisfactory substitute. We have got to do something to restore the sense of neighborhood in cities and to remove the feeling of anonymity which handicaps so many urban dwellers.

What we need to solve these and kindred problems is a new realization of civic and business duties. Against the all-embracing arm of government we must oppose the voluntary action of citizens, associated for the common good. Unless we do, we shall lose what we are fighting for, since as has well been said, "Liberty is possible only in a society where there are organizations other than political."

America does not want to become hag-ridden by doctrines that the state alone can save us. She will not become so merely because some converts to collectivist doctrines desire to snatch control away from the citizens. She can become so only if those who are responsible for all of the various private and community enterprises that make up our way of life abandon their responsibilities to government. The American is trained by tradition to admire individual achievement and to believe in the American pattern of individual opportunity. He will not change lightly. He wants to do a man's job in cooperation with his neighbors in the traditional American pattern. It is the duty of all who have enjoyed superior educational privileges to join in preserving that pattern. Business and government, along with all other agencies in American life, are under a joint compulsion to provide the basis for a good life on which the common man can build.

☆ ☆ ☆ ☆ ☆ ☆ ☆ ☆ ☆

IX. EDUCATION FOR USE

THE outbreak of war climaxed a decade of increasing unrest among the liberal arts colleges and many of their thoughtful friends. That the methods and results of higher education should be suffering criticism, internal as well as external, is to be taken as a wholesome sign of life and vigor. Were it otherwise the colleges would be surely dead.

As is customary in professional disputes, much of the discussion is directed to the body rather than the soul of the matter; in other words, to problems of structure and mechanism. Should the college course begin with the last two years of the secondary school and end with the sophomore year? Should the present four-year pattern be cut to three? Should the curriculum be classical and imposed, or should it be modern and free? Should students pass through college as rapidly as they can meet certain written examinations, or are there elements of personality and degrees of maturity that cannot be developed by this simple procedure?

Such questions, I know, raise some far-reaching considerations. I do not mean to depreciate their importance or the place that teaching techniques must occupy in the educational process. College teaching is a profession requiring its own special skills and methods, as much as any other profession; and this paper deals with some of them. But it is nevertheless always well to remember that over-emphasis on methods can obscure the basic necessity to do one's work well under whatever mechanisms adopted. We should always be on guard against the worship of educational gadgets; we should never permit preoccupation with technique to divert attention from the primary obligation to do an honest and enthusiastic job of teaching each day of the college year. The colleges are more open to criticism on the score of the proficiency with which they have used the tools they have chosen than in regard to the choice of tools they have elected to employ.

There is growing talk these days of the need to modify the college program to meet the changed social order which is to follow the war. If this means that the time has come to restudy the curriculum I agree wholeheartedly. But if it implies that we are to abandon the traditional concept of the liberal arts, the result will be wholly harmful. It is not the business of the college to prepare its students specifically for a new age, which the program-maker conceives to be approaching, but to equip a young person to stand on his feet in any age and to mold his age as his intelligence dictates. (There is always danger, too, that the new age may not arrive as scheduled.) Of course the content of the college curriculum must change from time to time. Some of it is out of date today because the subject matter as presented in college courses fails of its purpose or no longer fits the facts of life. The time has come for a re-examination of the curriculum, particularly in respect to the humanities and the social sciences, if our teaching is really to enter into the lives of our students. The urgent question, however, is not how we can adjust the college objectives to fit into a predicted social trend. The urgent matter before us is how can we attain more effectively those ends which have always been the goal of a liberal education. The chief emphasis should be on the quality of our work and the results we attain, on how we can do better what has been expected of us all along. There are few grounds for complacency over present accomplishments. There is patent room for improvement. Fortunately there is encouraging promise of improvement.

For the duration of the war, the normal objectives of the liberal arts colleges have been subordinated to the demands of military victory. The government's lack of tenderness toward them has evoked the criticism of educators and laymen alike. Some have not hesitated to declare that the government's policy will spell the end of the liberal arts colleges as America has known them. Such gospel of despair need not be taken seriously. If, as we believe, the subjects of college study deal with timeless values, such an assertion, if true, can only mean that our chief agency for preserving and cultivating these values has failed in its duty and ought to be put out of the way. For, as has been said, social institutions are not killed; they die and someone buries them. That the accident of war will destroy human curiosity and human aspirations which the colleges serve is an assertion which contradicts centuries of human experience. There are reasons for anticipating after the war a widespread revival of respect for the values of the spirit. Such revival will, however, have to contest the field with moral fatigue and crass materialism, and if the colleges are to give the full assistance of which they are capable they will have to be purged of sham and stripped of disabilities of which every conscientious educator is aware. A most hopeful sign is the fact that so many college faculties have already begun to take advantage of the opportunity which the war affords to restudy their methods and redefine their goals.

If the American liberal arts college is to play its part in contributing to democratic leadership, it will have to reduce the gap, too apparent in pre-war years, between its promise and its performance. It must see that its students understand more fully that the liberal arts are relevant to life; that a liberal education can and should be used.

We shall miss the point, however, if we succumb to pressure to do this through the instrumentality of vocational knowledge and special skills, rather than by emphasis on associative thinking and integration of humanistic and scientific knowledge. The mind trained to think, to carry on its own self-education, is, of course, a vocational asset. It will help its owner to a successful career, and it is scholastic snobbishness to insist that nothing useful should be studied in college. If college is a preparation for life it cannot afford to exclude a subject from the curriculum because it may contribute to earning a living. (Even the most intolerant classicist would not bar an undergraduate from his courses because he planned eventually to study for a Ph.D. and the subject matter might contribute, as it undoubtedly would, to his earning power in later years.) It is insincere to maintain that no vocational advantages should accrue from a liberal education.

The heightened value that a student finds in a subject which has some relation to his future career will usually, and quite properly, raise the quality of his work. But vocational interest must not set the tone of the college, whose prime objective is an educated person, not a skilled person. To illustrate by one example: a course in Labor Problems or Money and Banking is a proper element of a liberal arts curriculum; a course in real estate or salesmanship is not.

Associative thinking means the power to apply the experience and methods of analysis of one field to the problems of another; to build new patterns from the minutiae of experience which no stereotyped relation of cause and effect supplies. This is the highest achievement of the human intellect. It includes the power of thinking in abstract terms. True, abstractions are dangerous things when superficially grasped or heavily charged with emotion, but "the growth of the power of abstraction is precisely the growth of the human mind."

Experience shows that proficiency in one specialty does not of itself spell competence in another. It may happen that a learned scientist, for example, will talk folly when, with all the valor of ignorance, he applies his mind or his emotions to economics or sociology. Associative thinking (I realize that I am using the term loosely) is the process which builds the elements of special knowledge into social wisdom. We need to remind ourselves repeatedly that the man who is merely a specialist is a lop-sided individual. A liberal arts education is directed at one of the most fatal limitations of the human mind; namely, the tendency to concentrate on one segment of the chart of life and ignore the others. The consequence of this infirmity is distorted views and false, one-sided judgments.

The desired result at the college level cannot be attained by either paternal or professorial indoctrination, which means emphasis on pre-digested, secondhand ideas, as if an alert modern youth could be insulated from the electrically charged world about him. More than ever before, young people refuse to accept a hand-me-down faith. They insist upon thinking for themselves, and good teaching recognizes this by encouraging firsthand knowledge in which the student has a real sense of personal ownership. True, to intelligent young people who are starting to think for themselves the world is, as Taine remarked, a sorry place, but experience ripens judgment, and to inspire men to think for themselves is the only hope for the establishment of reason in a world of passion and violence. Harassed parents at times may envy Governor Berkeley who could say of Virginia in 1670: "I thank God there are no free schools, nor printing, for learning has brought disobedience and heresy into the world, and printing has divulged them." But the world long since ruled against the complacent governor; and free men are not afraid of heresy, nor do they reject the fruits of learning for fear that their complacency may be disturbed.

Since each person is a unique assortment of rational and nonrational urges (no one yet understands the myriad combinations which heredity supplies and which environment conditions) the college must emphasize the principle of individualization in its treatment of its students, both in respect to choices in the curriculum and association with the faculty. Although a measure of free electives of which the undergraduate can partake at will is desirable, his college career should not be aimless wandering through a curricular maze. The core of his college experience should be a planned and coherent program of study adjusted to his individual needs and capacities, and one which, by capitalizing the driving power of interest, will call forth the budding creative powers of his own mind. Only by individualizing the student and giving him a solid basis of related knowledge in one field on which his powers of original thought can play can we bring him to participate in his own education—and, as everyone knows, there is no substitute for participation. So far as the liberal arts course is concerned, mass education is a contradiction in terms. It is individuals we have to educate, not masses; and much of our educational waste flows from our failure to observe this practical truth.

While there can be no compromise with the college's first obligation to maintain high scholastic requirements, we who teach must remember that the impulse to think does not operate in a vacuum but in a setting of emotional impulses from which the thought process cannot be segregated but which must be in harmony with that process if it is to function satisfactorily. The American college, after the English model, has always accepted responsibility for the education of the emotions of its students. As Dr. Carrel has said, "The pure intellectual is an incomplete human being." Here is to be found the justification of the extra-curricular activities which the modern college supplies—often in too abundant quantities to the students who need them least, and with too little attention to those who need them most. Self-managed undergraduate activities, including properly managed sports (unfortunately too generally distorted in American colleges), have distinctly therapeutic values for the un-adjusted youth; for the normal student, they can expedite self-mastery and self-understanding. There is always danger, as Woodrow Wilson pointed out, that the side shows may swallow up the main tent, but if held within proper perspective they help to mature emotions and facilitate adjustment to one's fellows in an age in which nervous strain among youth is becoming a too prominent characteristic. I repeat, however, that if the primary job of intellectual training is not honestly and well performed the other influences which our colleges aim to exert will not avail. Athletics, social activities, and campus organizations should be entirely subordinate in the college program. If it fails in its primary professed function, which ought to distinguish it from other forms of voluntary associations, how can the college hope to accomplish the desirable collateral benefits?

Some educational spokesmen like to decry the "personality training" task of the college. It is true that a great deal of claptrap has been talked about character-building, as if it can be taught like mathematics or acquired as one learns to drive a car. Nevertheless the fact remains that the colleges do claim to develop personality, and as education is organized in the United States it is an inescapable part of their responsibility. But it cannot be done by special lectures and examinations. It is a by-product of daily work well performed. Youth is in somewhat the same condition as was primitive man, a bewildered stranger before the forces of nature and the turmoil of his own inward impulses. The young man coming to college feels the impact of an unfamiliar world at a time when he is biologically most upset by growing pains which he doesn't recognize or understand. One job of the college is to prepare youth to meet the world with a personality at harmony within itself; to render him firm in habits of moral conduct, not frustrated by inward warring tendencies nor at odds with the everchanging life around him. In this sense a liberal education is a liberating education, in that it should free a young person from emotional frustration and thus lead him to a release of his full intellectual potentialities. It should not generate colorless behavior but it should lead to balanced behavior; for it is a biological fact that life depends upon balance between the organism and its environment, and between the parts of the organism itself. If the individual is out of balance how can society maintain the harmony necessary to survival?

This is all true, and yet a calm appraisal will reveal that the conventional American college has been doing a better job at the personality level than at the intellectual. Extra-curricular activities have come nearer to fulfilling the claims made for them, than have the curricular and scholarly parts of a college experience. The balance should be restored. But Americans are still disposed to underrate scholarship, and too often colleges have weakly chosen to publicize the attractions of college life to the neglect of the claims of intellectual development and growth in knowledge. Indeed their greatest sin toward their students has been one of omission, their failure to expect enough of the student in the way of intellectual accomplishment during his four years on the campus. Reforms in this respect are in process and the present trend toward higher standards of work is revealing that the more we encourage a student to work and the more we demand of him, the more he works and the better he likes it. The opportunities for advanced work under special guidance which many colleges extend to the exceptional student, through honors courses or other methods of special treatment and programs of study which enable him to progress as fast as his capacities permit, are designed to work a belated justice to a group whose claims have been ignored too generally in the past. If faculties are too preoccupied with the average student, who after all represents the majority and as such is entitled to his share of attention, the rights of the better-than-average may easily be overlooked. Our duty to the latter is not discharged merely by giving him higher grades in the courses which all take and which tie the speedy runner with the men of more moderate accomplishments.

The colleges are under constant attack for failure to bridge the gap between theory and practice. Some of this criticism springs from a misunderstanding of what the colleges are for; some can be traced to lack of sympathy with the objective of a liberal arts education. Yet after due allowance for the mistaken views behind much of the popular criticism, a disquieting residuum remains.

There are two sides to a college education, and partisans of one are apt to depreciate the other. One is preparation for one's own personal happiness by enlarging one's world of ideas and by developing subjective appreciation of art, literature, history, and science. An education should enable a man to get more fun out of life, by giving him access to the broad empire of the mind where he can find a recuperative release from the restrictions of the work-a-day world. It is the life of the mind and the soul that sustains one in defeat and gives meaning to victory. But education misses the mark if it contributes only to one's own pleasure, no matter what level that pleasure attains. The danger is that the intellectual person, concentrating upon the inward look, will yield to the temptation to become merely an observer, good at protesting but poor in constructive attainment. If the educated person is a self-centered person, proud of his inflexible principles, opinionated and introspective, he will seek to avoid the citizen's responsibility for getting things done and to escape his share of the world's work. As Woodrow Wilson once said, "We are not put into this world to sit still and know; we are put here to act."

A liberal education should be an education for use. It not only should cultivate a desire in the student to apply his education to the world about him; it should also teach how he can so apply it. It is not enough to teach merely the content of the academic courses. How what is learned can be used must be taught also. Classroom training seeks to equip the student with certain techniques for solving problems and arriving at reasoned conclusions. These techniques, which we call the scientific method, strengthen the powers of analysis and synthesis, of weighing evidence and reporting conclusions. The classroom tries also to develop criteria of taste in art and literature, so that the student will come to appreciate beauty at its best, and to establish canons of what is ethically right or wrong for the individual and for society.

Now the subject matter and the methods of analysis and the criteria of judgment with which the classroom deals are equally useful and valid when applied to the actual situations of life. But the student may never become aware of this; he may never bridge the gap between learning about something in an academic way and applying his academic knowledge to the problems of later life. It is the function of the college not only to give him an education and exhort him to use it, but to teach him how to use it effectively. Many a college graduate has never truly realized that there is a blood relationship between the methods and subject matter of scholarship, to which he was exposed as a youth, and the practical job of being a happy and useful citizen. Unless the student is shown the way in college he may never relate what he absorbs from books to the world about him. Failure to do so helps to explain why so many college graduates read so few books.

The gap can be bridged only by affording opportunities for the student to participate in his own education and by seeing that he utilizes such opportunities. Only by so doing will his studies have a meaning for him.

Here some new methods are indicated which will cost money to apply. We have been willing to spend large sums on equipment and personnel for the physical sciences. The time has come to be more generous toward the reading subjects. The teaching of the physical sciences took a great leap forward when the laboratory was introduced and laboratory exercises became a normal part of a course in science. Similar success will attend the application of clinical methods to the teaching of the social sciences and inventive minds are engaged in experiments with similar devices in the humanities. The essential element is some method by which the student can apply his knowledge and methods of reasoning to a situation, new for him, yet one that he recognizes as part and parcel of the real world outside the classroom.

The social sciences in particular must emphasize education for use if they are to attain a vital influence. Because we who are teachers have overlooked this fact, the social sciences have failed to leave as vigorous an imprint on the minds of our students as they should. In stressing knowledge we have too often neglected participation. The consequence is that the technique of thinking and standards of judgment which the social sciences seek to supply are not carried over into the sphere of practical application where their ultimate values lie. Aristotle complained that the Sophists while professing to teach statesmanship were plainly a long way off from doing so because not one of them practiced it, nor did any of them make statesmen of their sons or their friends. Practice, however, he adds, seems to contribute no little to the acquisition of the faculty of statesmanship. In the term "practice" we may include all possible methods for introducing participation into the educational process at the college level.

Much the same criticism can be made for the teaching of the humanities. While insisting that the humanities prepare for life, we have been teaching them too generally as subjects remote from life, expecting the student by his unaided efforts to make the transfer from the classroom to life by some mysterious process which we have been too ignorant to explain or inculcate. The consequence is that too often the transfer is never made, even in the life of the teacher, because the gap is never bridged. What is taught in the classroom remains in the "classroom compartment" of a young man's mind because he has never been taught how to use it.

I have stressed the job yet to be done because of the new opportunities that will confront the American college in the post-war days of demobilization and reconstruction. Because of its geographical position, America will suffer least from the war. By reason of this fact she seems destined to become one of the chief conservators of the cultural attainments of the human race. Upon the American liberal arts college, therefore, will fall a major obligation to sustain those values of the human will and spirit which comprise what we call civilization.

It is not likely that we shall repeat this time the mistake of thinking that democracy can be imposed overnight on other peoples who have had little experience with self-government and perhaps have less desire for it. Nevertheless we are justified in believing that democracy is the best instrument for "activating" the ideals of Western Civilization and in hoping that peoples who do not now know democracy may come to want it. How much they will desire to do so will depend on the example provided by existing democracies and particularly by our own. International questions, therefore, will be affected quite as much as domestic problems by the degree to which we make democracy work in our own country. The liberal arts college is dedicated to the education of the whole man. It deals with those human elements and human relations which alone can provide a world "language" for building unity and harmony among nations. We cannot organize nations around new gadgets for automobiles; we can organize them around ideas.

That acute Russian critic of democracy, Berdyaev, tells us that democracy was in crisis before the war because it emphasized the freedom of the individual to choose without setting up any standards of choice. Because they were thus deprived of a spiritual purpose, democracies were, he believes, staggering blindly. A mechanical counting of votes, he rightly asserts, will not lead to good results if those who cast their ballots have lost sight of truth.

I believe it is true that democracy has through concentration on counting ballots neglected the search for organic truth. I do not mean to suggest that we give up the ballot box as the arbiter of public policy—it was a great invention—but I do mean to insist that we take pains that its verdict be true. Unless the issues which the ballot box adjudicates are relevant and the major decisions sound, free elections will sooner or later be discarded in favor of something else much less effective in the long run.

Programs of social action do not bubble up of themselves from undifferentiated mobs. Programs have to be made; they are conceived by the few and accepted by the many. Democracy cannot lift its mass weight by its own bootstraps. It needs leaders who can raise us to heights we should not otherwise attain, but they must be responsible leaders, not bosses. The problem of democracy thus resolves itself into the age-old problem of leadership, and by leadership I do not mean merely the services of the selected few who achieve national prominence and newspaper headlines, important though they be. Democracy cannot dispense with distinguished men but it will not be saved by reliance on Napoleonic personalities. It must have community leaders, neighborhood leaders, as well. Every man—he may be the keeper of a crossroads country store—whom his neighbors trust and follow is a leader.

The agency at hand best fitted to infuse into society a constant leaven of leadership motivated by an understanding of science, history and the arts is the American college. Without men in posts of leadership sensitive to the values of those subjects, our free society as we know it will crumble. True, there are many such who have never had the opportunity of a college education, but the country cannot rely upon a casual supply of broadly educated people. It must act positively to develop them and the best instrumentality at hand is the non-vocational college.

Here is a responsibility that will demand the best that we can offer. It will call for a continuation of the high objectives of liberal education and for a far better realization of these objectives—for a performance that will plumb the still latent possibilities of the American college.

The Material for the Foregoing Essays
Was Taken from the Following Addresses:

☆

I. TRUSTEES OF THE AMERICAN DREAM
Commencement Address, January 29, 1943

II. COMING: AN AGE OF FRESH OPPORTUNITY
1942 Baccalaureate Address

III. TOWARD A DURABLE PEACE
Commencement Address, May 29, 1943

IV. THE ANATOMY OF COURAGE
1941 Baccalaureate Address

V. FREEDOM *and* RESPONSIBILITY
1940 Baccalaureate Address

VI. THE CASE FOR LIBERALISM
1936 Baccalaureate Address

VII. "HE THAT'S SECURE IS NOT SAFE"
1937 Baccalaureate Address

VIII. DEMOCRACY'S CHALLENGE TO PRIVATE AND
COMMUNITY ENTERPRISE
Address at Princeton Conference on Post-War Problems, April, 1943

IX. EDUCATION FOR USE
Various Addresses before Educational Groups